TO SPACE & BACK

TO SPACE & BACK

By Sally Ride with Susan Okie

A BEECH TREE PAPERBACK BOOK
NEW YORK

FOR
DR. ELIZABETH MOMMAERTS
AND IN MEMORY OF ASTRONAUTS
DICK SCOBEE
MIKE SMITH
JUDY RESNIK
RON McNAIR
ELLISON ONIZUKA
GREGORY JARVIS
CHRISTA McAULIFFE

Title page photograph: Looking east through the Straits of Gibraltar into the Mediterranean Sea. To the left is Spain, to the right is Africa.

First Beech Tree edition, 1991

7 9 10 8 6

Library of Congress Cataloging in Publication Data
Ride, Sally. To space and back.
Summary: Describes in text and photographs what it is like to be an astronaut on the space shuttle. Includes a glossary of terms.
1. Space flight—Juvenile literature.   2. Space shuttles—Juvenile literature.   [1. Space flight   2. Space shuttles]   I. Okie, Susan.
II. Title.   TL793.R536   1986   629.45′4′0924   85-23757   ISBN 0-688-09112-1 (pbk)

TO SPACE & BACK

"What's it like to be in space?" "Is it scary?" "Is it cold?" "Do you have trouble sleeping?" These are questions that everyone asks astronauts who have been in space. The experience is hard to describe. The words and pictures in this book will help you imagine what it's like to blast off in a rocket and float effortlessly in midair while circling hundreds of miles above the Earth.

My first space flight was in June 1983, with four other astronauts: Bob Crippen, Rick Hauck, John Fabian, and Norm Thagard. We went up in the space shuttle, the world's first spaceplane, which carries all of today's astronauts into space. We blasted off from a launch pad in Florida; then we circled the Earth for seven days. As we went around and around the planet, we launched two satellites, studied the Earth, and learned about weightlessness. After a week in orbit we returned to Earth. Our adventure ended as the space shuttle glided back through the atmosphere to a smooth landing in California.

Crip, Rick, John, Norm, and I have each had a chance to visit space again. We have found time on every trip to relax, enjoy weightlessness, and admire the view of the Earth and the stars. And, like all astronauts, we have found time to take pictures. The pictures help us to capture the excitement of our trip into space and share the adventure with our friends when we get back.

Most of the photographs in this book were taken by

Left to right: Bob Crippen, Sally Ride, Norm Thagard, Rick Hauck, John Fabian.

astronauts on board the space shuttle. Some were taken on my flights, some on other space shuttle flights. They will show you what it's like to eat from a spoon floating in midair, to put on a spacesuit for a walk in space, and to gaze at the Earth's oceans far below.

When I was growing up, I was always fascinated by the planets, stars, and galaxies, but I never thought about becoming an astronaut. I studied math and science in high school, and then I spent my years in college learning physics—the study of the laws of nature and the universe. Just as I was finishing my education, NASA, the United States space agency, began looking for scientists who wanted to become astronauts. Suddenly I knew that I wanted a chance to see the Earth and the stars from outer space. I sent my application to NASA, and after a series of tests and interviews, I was chosen to be an astronaut.

On January 28, 1986, this book was almost ready to go to the printer, when the unthinkable happened. The space shuttle *Challenger* exploded one minute after lift-off. After the accident I thought a lot about the book, and whether or not I wanted to change any part of it. I decided that nothing except the dedication and the words I write here should be changed.

I wrote this book because I wanted to answer some of the questions that young people ask of astronauts. Many of the questions are about feelings, and one that now may have added meaning is, "Is it scary?"

All adventures—especially into new territory—are scary, and there has always been an element of danger in space flight. I wanted to be an astronaut because I thought it would be a challenging opportunity. It was; it was also an experience that I shall never forget.

—Sally Ride

This split view of the nose of the space shuttle shows the flight deck and mid-deck areas, which are the living and working quarters for the crew. The much roomier cargo bay carries satellites and other equipment involved with the shuttle's mission. The cargo bay doors are always open while the shuttle is in orbit. The airlock hatch located on the mid-deck gives the crew access to the cargo bay.

cargo bay | crew quarters

Drawing by Mike Eagle

A pilot seat
B commander seat
C flight deck
D mid-deck
E ladder
F interdeck access
G robot arm controls
H experiment and
   satellite control station
I airlock
J airlock hatch

K personal hygiene area
L side hatch
M sleeping bags
N stowage areas and food pantry
O fire extinguisher
P foot loop
Q window
R space shuttle controls
S exercise treadmill
T computer terminals
   and keyboards

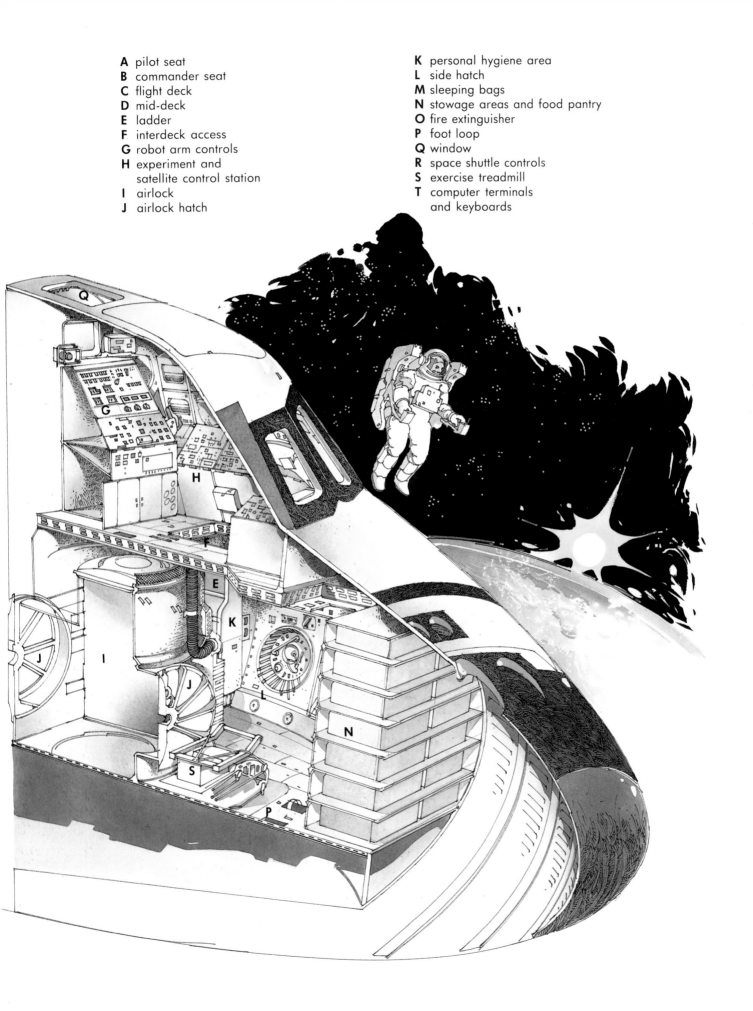

Floodlights brighten the early morning departure of an astronaut crew on their way to the launch pad.

12

LAUNCH MORNING.

6 . . . 5 . . . 4 . . .

The alarm clock counts down.

3 . . . 2 . . . 1 . . .

Rrring! 3:15 A.M. *Launch minus four hours.* Time to get up.

It's pitch black outside. In four hours a space shuttle launch will light up the sky.

Nine miles from the launch pad, in the astronaut crew quarters, we put on our flight suits, get some last-minute information, and eat a light breakfast.

Launch minus three hours. It's still dark. We leave the crew quarters, climb into the astronaut van, and head for the launch pad.

The space shuttle stands with its nose pointed toward the sky, attached to the big orange fuel tank and two white rockets that will lift it—and us—into space.

The spotlights shining on the space shuttle light the last part of our route. Although we're alone, we know that thousands of people are watching us now, during the final part of the countdown.

When we step out onto the pad, we're dwarfed by the thirty-story-high space shuttle. Our spaceplane looked peaceful from the road, but now we can hear it hissing and gurgling as though it's alive.

The long elevator ride up the launch tower takes us to a level near the nose of the space shuttle, 195 feet above the ground. Trying hard not to look down at the pad far below, we walk out onto an access arm and into the "white room." The white room, a small white chamber at the end of the movable walkway, fits right next to the space shuttle's hatch. The only other people on the launch pad—in fact, the only other people for miles—are the six technicians waiting for us in the white room. They help us put on our escape harnesses and launch helmets and help us climb through the hatch. Then they strap us into our seats.

Because the space shuttle is standing on its tail, we are lying on our backs as we face the nose. It's awkward to twist around to look out the windows. The commander has a good view of the launch tower, and the pilot has a good view of the Atlantic Ocean, but no one else can see much outside.

Launch minus one hour. We check to make sure that we are strapped in properly, that oxygen will flow into our helmets, that our radio communication with Mission Control is working, and that our pencils and our books—the procedure manuals and checklists we'll need during liftoff—are attached to something to keep them from shaking loose. Then we wait.

The technicians close the hatch and then head for safety three miles away. We're all alone on the launch pad.

Launch minus seven minutes. The walkway with the white room at the end slowly pulls away. Far below us

Space shuttle *Discovery* poised on the launch pad.

the power units start whirring, sending a shudder through the shuttle. We close the visors on our helmets and begin to breathe from the oxygen supply. Then the space shuttle quivers again as its launch engines slowly move into position for blast-off.

Launch minus 10 seconds . . . 9 . . . 8 . . . 7 . . . The three launch engines light. The shuttle shakes and strains at the bolts holding it to the launch pad. The computers check the engines. It isn't up to us any-more—the computers will decide whether we launch.

3 . . . 2 . . . 1 . . . The rockets light! The shuttle leaps off the launch pad in a cloud of steam and a trail of fire. Inside, the ride is rough and loud. Our heads are rat-tling around inside our helmets. We can barely hear the voices from Mission Control in our headsets above the thunder of the rockets and engines. For an instant I wonder if everything is working right. But there's no more time to wonder, and no time to be scared.

In only a few seconds we zoom past the clouds. Two minutes later the rockets burn out, and with a brilliant whitish-orange flash, they fall away from the shuttle as it streaks on toward space. Suddenly the ride becomes very, very smooth and quiet. The shuttle is still attached to the big tank, and the launch engines are pushing us out of Earth's atmosphere. The sky is black. All we can see of the trail of fire behind us is a faint, pulsating glow through the top window.

Launch plus six minutes. The force pushing us against the backs of our seats steadily increases. We can barely move because we're being held in place by a force of 3 g's—three times the force of gravity we feel on Earth. At first we don't mind it—we've all felt much more than that when we've done acrobatics in our jet training airplanes. But that lasted only a few seconds, and this seems to go on forever. After a couple of minutes of 3 g's, we're uncomfortable, straining to hold our books on our laps and craning our necks against the force to read the instruments. I find myself wishing we'd hurry up and get into orbit.

Launch plus eight and one-half minutes. The launch engines cut off. Suddenly the force is gone, and we lurch forward in our seats. During the next few minutes the empty fuel tank drops away and falls to Earth, and we are very busy getting the shuttle ready to enter orbit. But we're not too busy to notice that our books and pencils are floating in midair. We're in space!

42

Looking east across Wales and England. The English Channel is at lower right, Cardigan Bay and the Bristol Channel to the left.

20

The atmosphere thins gradually as we travel farther from Earth. At fifty miles up, we're above most of the air, and we're officially "in space." We aren't in orbit yet, though, and without additional push the shuttle would come crashing back to Earth.

We use the shuttle's smaller space engines to get us into our final, safe orbit about two hundred miles above Earth. In that orbit we are much higher than airplanes, which fly about six miles up, but much lower than weather satellites, which circle Earth more than twenty-two thousand miles up.

Once we are in orbit, our ride is very peaceful. The engines have shut down, and the only noise we hear is the hum of the fans that circulate our air. We are traveling at five miles a second, going around the Earth once every ninety minutes, but we don't feel the motion. We can't even tell we're moving unless we look out the window at Earth.

We stay much closer to home than the astronauts who flew space capsules to the moon in 1969. When those astronauts stood on the moon, they described the distant Earth as a big blue-and-white marble suspended in space. We are a long way from the moon, and we never get far enough from Earth to see the whole planet at once.

We still have a magnificent view. The sparkling blue oceans and bright orange deserts are glorious against the blackness of space. Even if we can't see the whole planet, we can see quite a distance. When we are over Los Angeles we can see as far as Oregon; when we are over Florida we can see New York.

The Swiss, French, and Italian Alps.

We see mountain ranges reaching up to us and canyons falling away. We see huge dust storms blowing over deserts in Africa and smoke spewing from the craters of

22

This hurricane is hundreds of miles across.

active volcanoes in Hawaii. We see enormous chunks of ice floating in the Antarctic Ocean and electrical storms raging over the Atlantic.

23

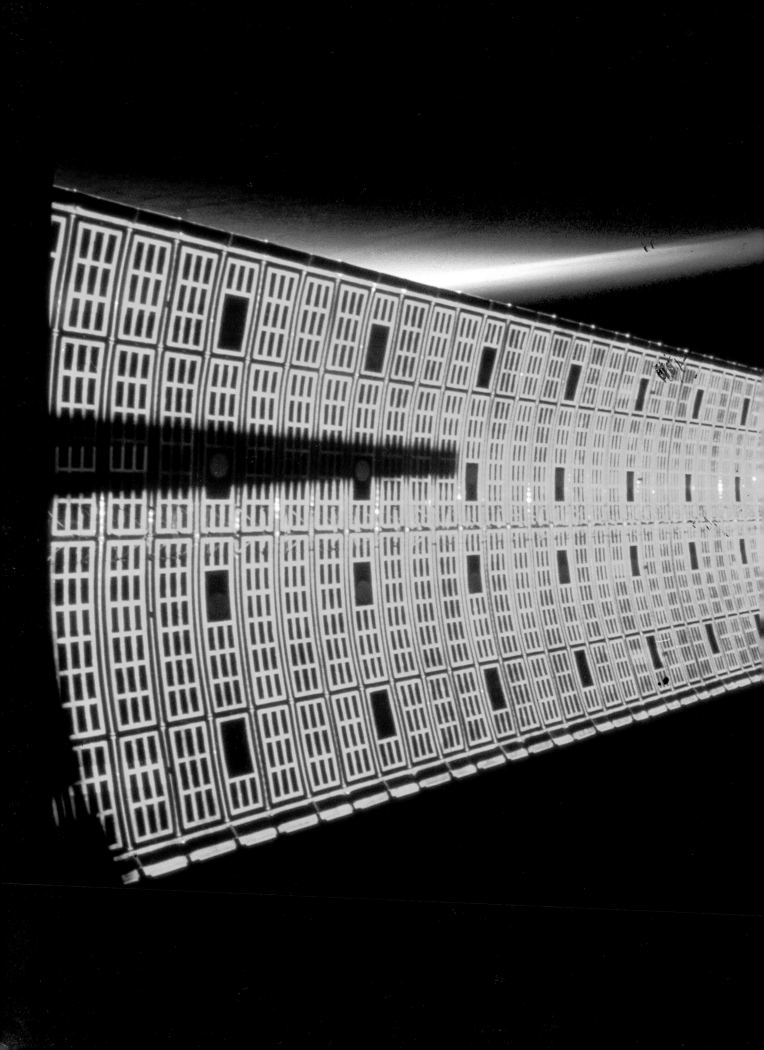

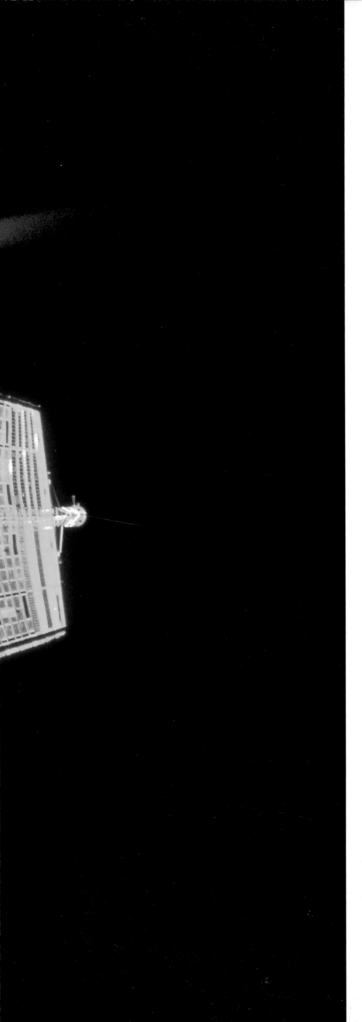

Sunrises and sunsets are spectacular from orbit. Since we see one sunrise and one sunset each time we go around the Earth, we can watch sixteen sunrises and sixteen sunsets every twenty-four hours. Our sightseeing doesn't stop while we are over the dark side of the planet. We can see twinkling city lights, the reflection of the moon in the sea, and flashes of lightning from thunderstorms.

This solar array panel was photographed by an astronaut inside the shuttle just as the spacecraft headed toward a sunrise.

25

These natural features are not the only things we can see. We can also spot cities, airport runways, bridges, and other signs of civilization. When our orbit takes us over

The Houston area. The circled spot near the bottom is the NASA Lyndon B. Johnson Space Center, which is where I work most of the time.

Florida, we are even able to see the launch pad at Cape Canaveral, where we crawled into the space shuttle just hours earlier.

The New York City area. The Hudson River, with New Jersey and the Delaware Water Gap to its left, empties into New York Harbor at right.

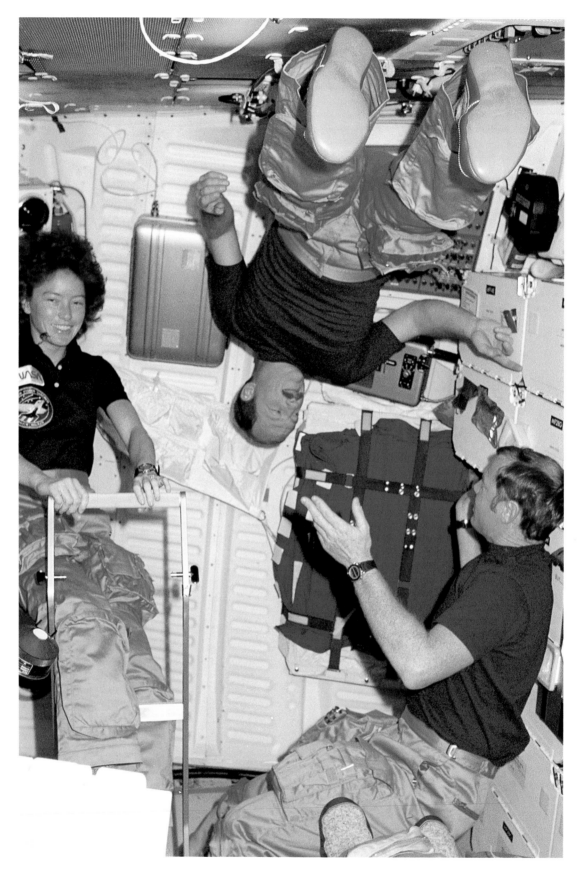

THE BEST PART OF BEING IN SPACE IS BEING WEIGHTLESS. It feels wonderful to be able to float without effort; to slither up, down, and around the inside of the shuttle just like a seal; to be upside down as often as I'm right side up and have it make no difference. On Earth being upside down feels different because gravity is pulling the blood toward my head. In space I feel exactly the same whether my head is toward the floor or toward the ceiling.

When I'm weightless, some things don't change. My heart beats at about the same rate as it does on Earth. I can still swallow and digest food. My eyes, ears, nose, and taste buds work fine; I see, hear, smell, and taste things just as I do at home.

I *look* a little different, though—all astronauts do. Since the fluid in our bodies is not pulled toward our feet as it is on Earth, more of this fluid stays in our faces and upper bodies. This makes our faces a little fatter and gives us puffy-looking cheeks. We are also about an inch taller while in orbit because in weightlessness our spines are not compressed. Unfortunately (for me, anyway), we shrink back to normal height when we return to Earth.

During my first day in space, I had to learn how to move around. I started out trying to "swim" through the air, but that didn't work at all; air isn't dense, the way water is, and I felt silly dog-paddling in the air, going nowhere. Before long I discovered that I had to push

Anna Fisher, Rick Hauck, and Dave Walker floating, weightless.

Joe Allen has let a big ball of orange juice out of his drink container. He's using a straw to guide it around the room. He could use that straw to drink it out of midair if he wanted to!

off from one of the walls if I wanted to get across the room. At first I would push off a little too hard and crash into the opposite wall, but I soon learned to wind my way around with very gentle pushes.

In weightlessness the slightest touch can start an astronaut's body floating across the room or drifting over in a slow-motion somersault. The only way to stop moving is to take hold of something that's anchored in place. Early in my first flight I constantly felt that I was about to lose control, as though I were teetering on a balance beam or tipping over in a canoe. It's a strange, unsteady feeling that's difficult to describe, but fortunately it goes away. After a day or two I got the knack of staying still and could change clothes without tumbling backward.

Jeff Hoffman and Rhea Seddon brought a Slinky along to see how well it would "slink" in weightlessness.

Some astronauts are uncomfortable while their bodies are adjusting to weightlessness. Almost half of all shuttle crew members are sick for the first day or two. Space sickness is not like the motion sickness caused by bobbing on a boat or riding a roller coaster. It affects each person differently. A space-sick astronaut might feel nauseated or tired or disoriented or just strange. So far we haven't found out exactly what causes space sickness or how to cure it.

By the third day of a week-long shuttle flight, though, all the astronauts are feeling fine. Weightlessness is pure fun, once everyone gets the hang of it. The two rooms inside the shuttle seem much larger than they do on Earth, because we are not held down to the floor. We can use every corner of a room, including the ceiling. While one of us works strapped to a wall, another sits on the ceiling eating peanuts, and a third runs on a treadmill anchored to the floor. On Earth we need a ladder to climb from the mid-deck to the flight deck. In space we never use the ladder—we just float from one room to another.

One person's upside down is another person's right side up. I'm coming down—head first—from the flight deck, while Kathy Sullivan is on her way up. The ladder that I have my hand on is completely useless in space.

32

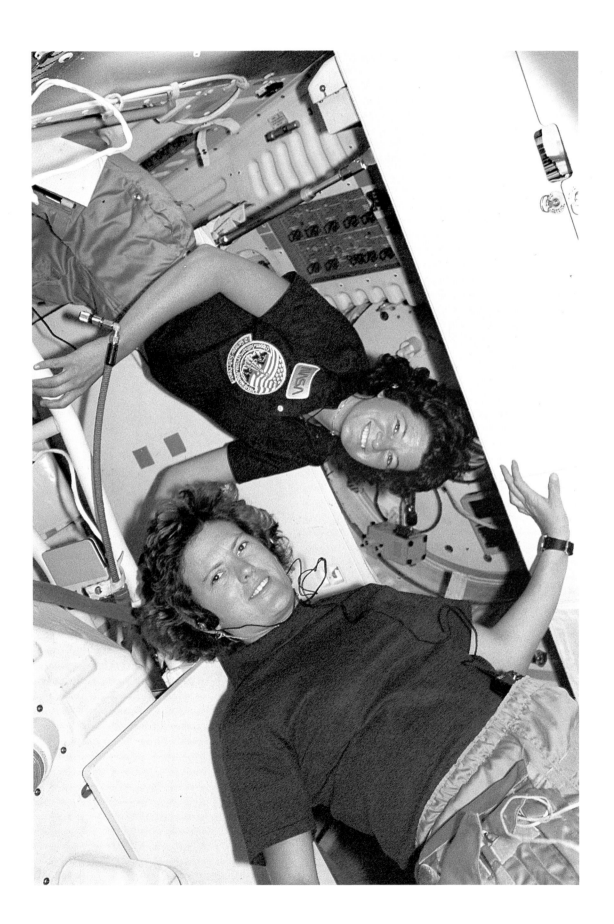

For the first day or two in space, most astronauts are not as hungry as they would be on the ground. But by the third day, almost everyone has regained a normal appetite, and some—like me—actually eat a little more than usual.

Eating feels the same as it does on Earth. It's just as easy to swallow food and drink water in space, and everything tastes about the same as it would on Earth. Some of the food we carry on the space shuttle is like what we would eat at home: bread, tuna, canned pudding, apples, carrots, peanuts, and cookies. We also have soups, vegetables, and main courses like chicken-and-noodle casserole, but these are freeze-dried and vacuum-packed in individual plastic cartons.

Astronauts eat three meals a day and take turns preparing food. Usually one or two astronauts make a meal for the whole crew.

Sometimes I ate sitting on the ceiling.

To fix lunch, here's what an astronaut has to do:

1. Open the food locker and see what has been planned for lunch. How about hot dogs, macaroni and cheese, peanuts, and lemonade?

2. Get out the food trays. Each crewmember has a tray that has slots to hold the cartons in place.

3. Attach the trays to the wall with Velcro so they won't float away.

4. Put one package of peanuts in each food tray.

5. Turn on the oven, open the oven door, and slide in the hot dogs in their sealed foil bags.

6. Fit the cartons of dehydrated macaroni and cheese, one at a time, into the water dispenser. The dispenser pushes a needle into the carton and squirts in the right amount of water.

7. Squeeze each macaroni carton to mix in the water, and then place it in the oven too.

8. Use the water dispenser to add water to each plastic carton of powdered lemonade. Slide a straw into each carton and put one lemonade carton in each tray.

9. Remove the hot food from the oven and put a carton of macaroni and a pouch of hot dogs in each tray.

10. Get out bread, butter, catsup, and mustard. Crewmembers have to make their own hot-dog sandwiches; once a sandwich is made, it can't be put down because it would float apart.

11. Call the rest of the crew to "come and get it." We gather on the mid-deck to enjoy meals together like a family. The engineers at Mission Control try not to call us while we're eating, so we have some time to talk to

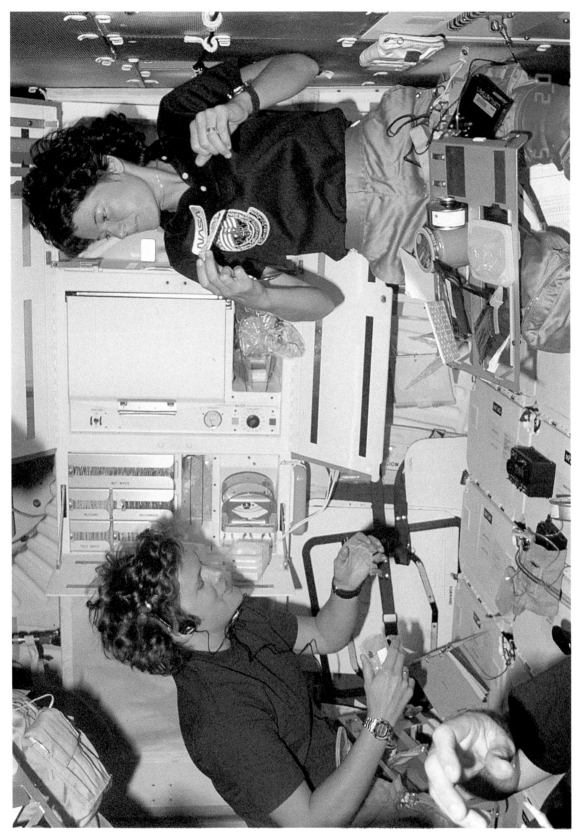

Believe it or not: Kathy Sullivan and I are dining "right side up."

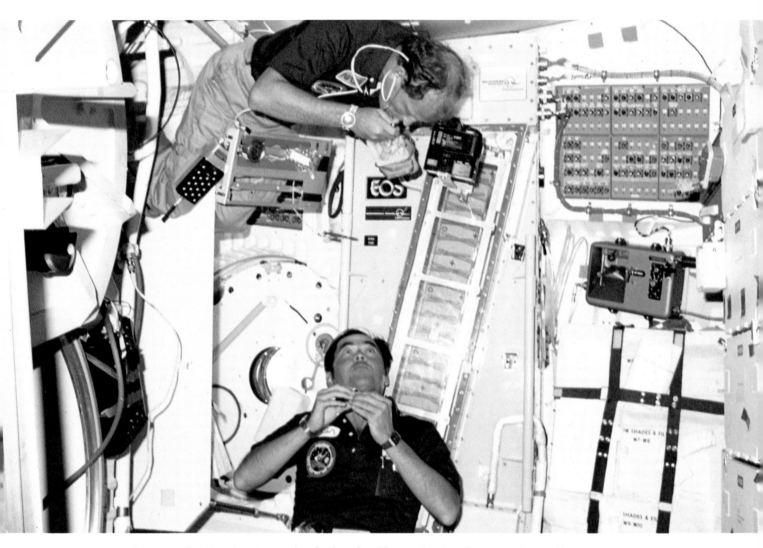

Left: It's Dale Gardner's turn to fix lunch. *Above:* None of Norm Thagard's macaroni and cheese will fall on Bob Crippen's head—even if it slips off the spoon.

one another and relax. But we don't look like a family sitting down to lunch on Earth. We don't eat at a table; our tables are the trays strapped to our legs. We don't sit in chairs. Each of us finds a comfortable spot—maybe floating near the ceiling, or upside down in the middle of the cabin.

We each have a knife and fork, but our most useful pieces of silverware are spoons and scissors. We need scissors to snip open the foil pouches of hot dogs, the packages of peanuts, and the plastic cartons of macaroni.

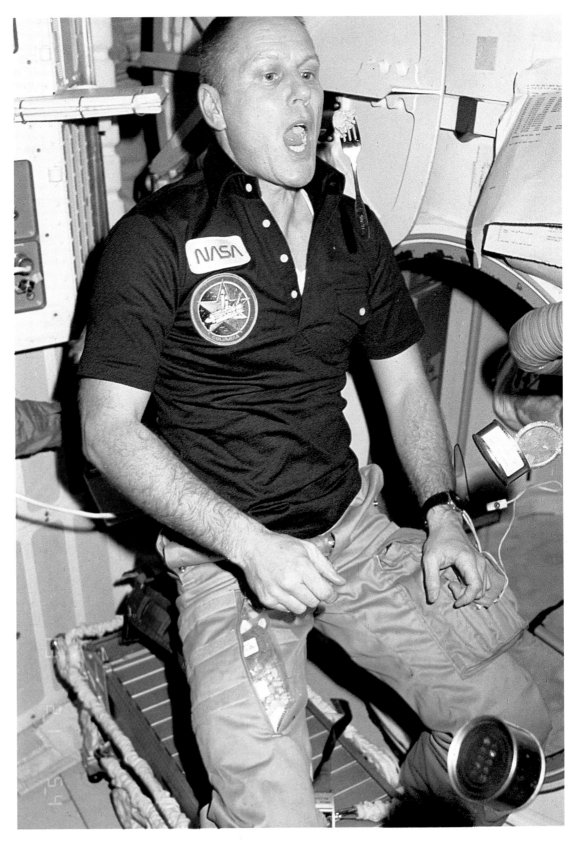

Bob Overmyer eating—no hands!

Then we use spoons to get the food to our mouths. Most of our food is deliberately made sticky enough to stay on a spoon and not float away as we try to eat it. In fact, we can flip our spoons all the way across the cabin and the food won't come off—usually! Sometimes a blob of pudding escapes from a spinning spoon, and we have to catch it before it splatters on a wall.

A few foods, like scrambled eggs, are not quite sticky enough to stay on a spoon. I quickly learned to hold the carton close to my mouth and use my spoon to aim each bite of egg.

We don't have drinking glasses. If we tipped a glass of milk to drink from it, nothing would happen—the weightless milk would stay in the glass. We have to use straws to suck our drinks out of cartons.

Don Williams and Bo Bobko juggling.

We don't use salt shakers either, because grains of salt would float around the cabin instead of falling on the food. To solve this problem, we squeeze liquid salt into the cartons and then mix it with the food.

A peanut-butter sandwich is simple to fix on Earth, but in space it takes two astronauts to prepare one. The first time I tried to make a peanut-butter sandwich, I held the jar of peanut butter, unscrewed the top, and found I needed another hand. If I let go of either the lid or the jar, it would float away. So I tossed the lid to another astronaut and picked up a knife—but with the jar in one hand and the knife in the other, I had no way to reach for the bread! After that I asked someone else to hold the bread or the jar whenever I wanted a sandwich.

Astronauts can't always resist the fun of playing with weightless food. On one of my flights, we set a cookie floating in the middle of the room and then "flew" an astronaut, with his mouth wide open, across the cabin to capture it. We often share bags of peanuts because it gives us an excuse to play catch, floating peanuts back and forth into each other's mouths. We race to capture spinning carrots and bananas and practice catching spoonfuls of food in our mouths while they twirl in mid-air. These tricks are easy in space, but I don't recommend trying them on Earth.

After meals we clean up. We simply wipe off whatever utensils have been used and stow them in our pockets. Since each serving of food comes in its own carton, can, or pouch, "washing the dishes" really means disposing of the trash. We pack our empty food containers into garbage bags and bring all our trash back to Earth with us.

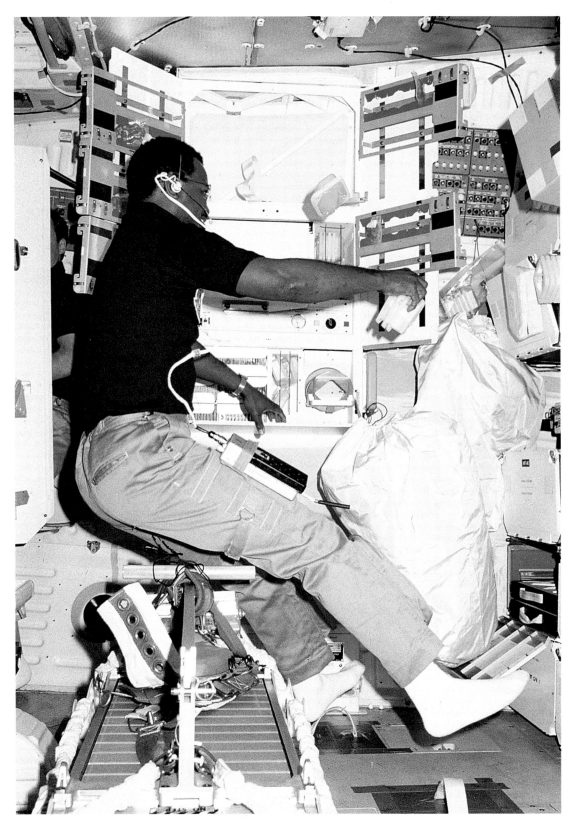

It's Ron McNair's turn to collect all the cartons and stuff them into a trash bag that floats near the kitchen.

We don't have beds in the space shuttle, but we do have sleeping bags. Unlike the kind used on camping trips, each of these bags has a stiff pad for body support, a thin bag that can be unzipped from the pad and used by itself, and a pillow. During the day, when we're working, we leave the bags tied to the wall, out of the way. At bedtime we untie them and take them wherever we've chosen to sleep.

On most space shuttle flights everyone sleeps at the same time. No one has to stay awake to watch over the spaceplane; the shuttle's computers and the engineers at Mission Control do that. If anything were to go wrong, the computers would ring an alarm and the engineers would call us on the radio.

On board the space shuttle, sleep-time doesn't mean nighttime. During each ninety-minute orbit the sun "rises" and shines brilliantly through our windows for about fifty minutes; then it "sets" as our path takes us around to the dark side of Earth. Forty minutes later the sun "rises" again as we return to the daylight side of the globe. So sunlight pours through the space shuttle windows more than half the time while we're trying to rest. To keep the sun out of our eyes, we wear black sleep masks, which we call Lone Ranger masks.

It is surprisingly easy to get comfortable and fall asleep in space. Every astronaut sleeps differently. Some sleep upside down, some sideways, some right side up. Some crawl into their sleeping bags and then tie them to anything handy, to keep them floating in one place. Others use the thin bags alone as blankets and wedge

Richard Truly and Guy Bluford have folded their arms and crossed their ankles to keep their arms and legs from floating out in front of them while they sleep.

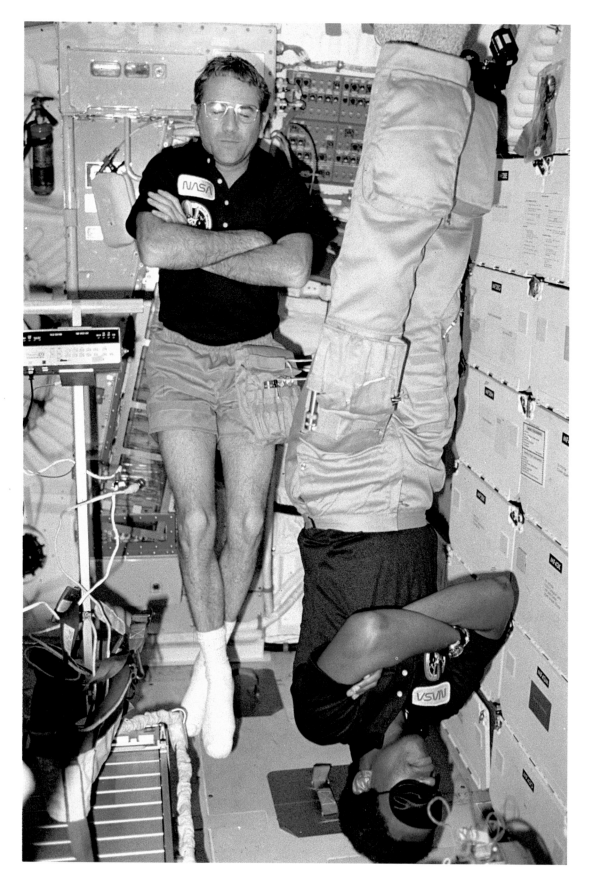

themselves into corners. Still others simply float in the middle of the cabin, sometimes cushioning their heads in case they drift gently against the ceiling—or another sleeping astronaut.

The first time I tried to sleep while weightless, I discovered that my arms and legs moved automatically into a "sleep position." Instead of hanging at my sides, as they would on Earth, my arms drifted out in front of me, motionless, at about shoulder height. It was strange to open my eyes and see my arms dangling in front of my face.

I also found that I couldn't turn over in space. There was no such thing as lying on my back, on my side, or on my stomach—it was all the same. No matter how much I twisted and turned, my body would go back to exactly the same natural sleep position as soon as I relaxed.

I don't use my pillow because I have discovered that my head will not stay on it unless I strap it there. I don't use the stiff pad, either—just the light bag. When it's time to sleep, I gather my bag, my sleep mask, and my tape player with earphones and float up to the flight deck. Then I crawl into the bag, zip it around me, and float in a sort of sitting position just above a seat, right next to a window. Before I pull the mask down over my eyes, I relax for a while, listening to music and watching the Earth go by beneath me.

When I'm in orbit it seems as though I don't need quite as much sleep as I do on Earth. Maybe that's because when I am weightless I don't use my muscles as much, so I don't feel as tired. Or maybe it's because I'm excited to be in space and don't want to waste time sleeping.

Some astronauts leave their sleeping bags attached to the wall and climb into them to sleep. Anna Fisher is resting, floating inside her sleeping bag.

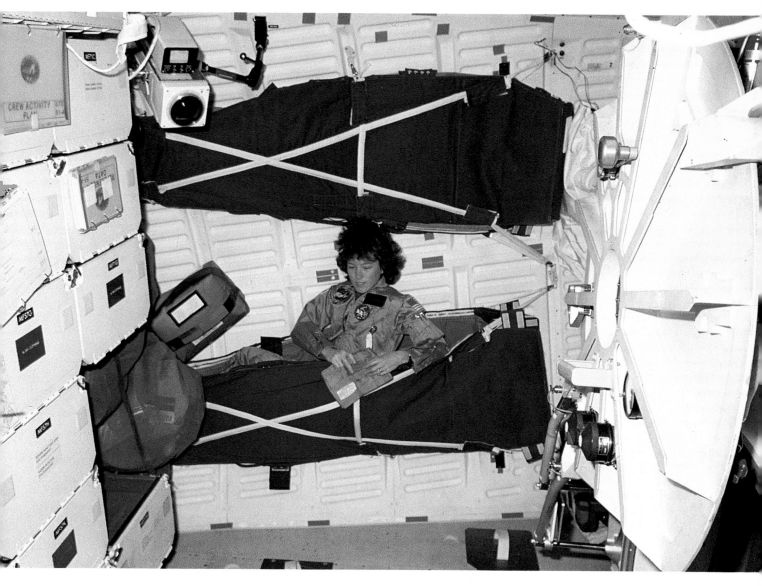

I start each day on the space shuttle just as I do on Earth: I wash my face, brush my teeth, comb my hair, and use the toilet. In space my usual way of doing all these things is different because water, toothpaste, hair, and body wastes are weightless.

On the spaceplane we don't have a sink, bathtub, or shower because water coming out of a faucet would float in little blobs all over the cabin. Instead, we have a water gun, a hose with a trigger control on the nozzle. I put a

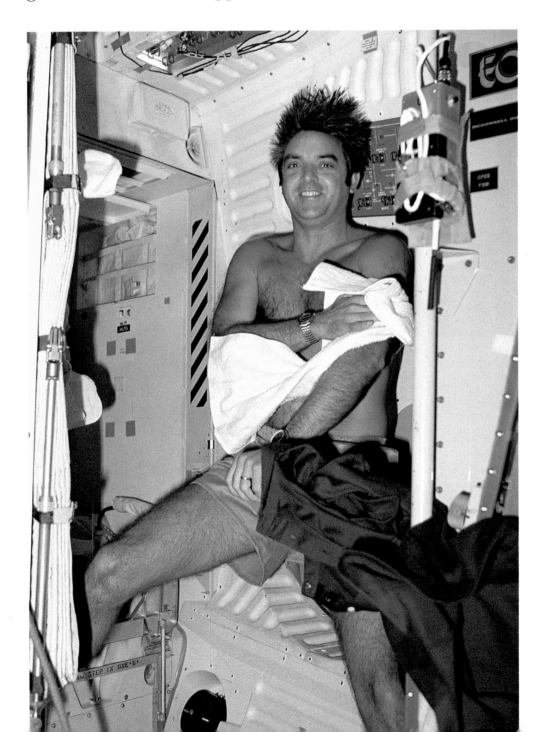

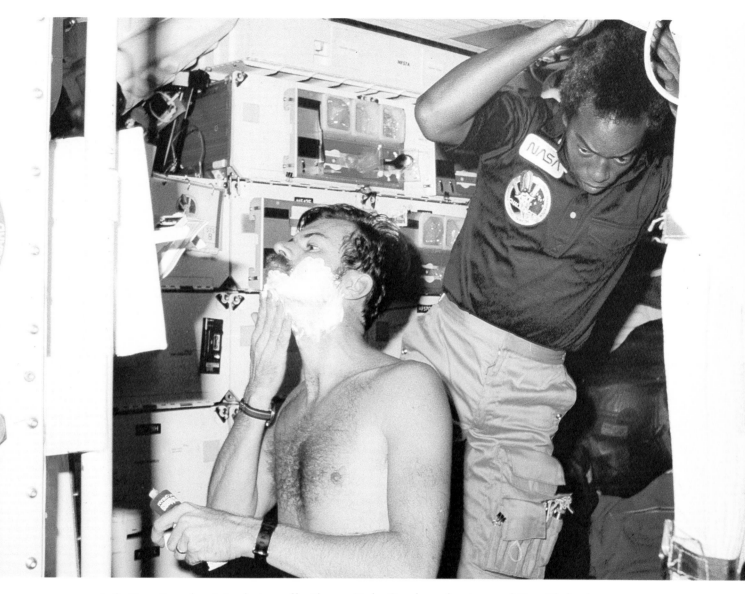

Left: Dan Brandenstein drying off. *Above:* Dale Gardner shaving and Guy Bluford floating past.

washcloth next to the nozzle and wet it; then I use it with soap to wash my hands and face.

The men find shaving easier than it might appear. Whiskers don't float away—they stick to the shaving cream, and the shaving cream sticks to the razor. After an astronaut finishes shaving, he wipes the razor clean with a wet washcloth. Electric razors work too: the whiskers are sucked into the razor after they're shaved off.

The toothbrush I use looks ordinary, but it has special digestible toothpaste already in the bristles. I have to swallow the toothpaste because I can't spit it into a sink (remember, there is no sink). Every morning I unwrap a new toothbrush, use it, swallow the toothpaste, and throw the brush away.

I brush and comb my hair just as I would on Earth, but it doesn't do much good; my weightless hair still floats around my head.

There is a special space toilet on board the shuttle in a small closet built into one wall of the cabin. The toilet has a contoured seat over a bowl, and connected to it is a long, flexible tube with a removable cone-shaped urine cup at the end. (Each astronaut has a personal cup that fits onto the tube.) To use the urine cup, I hold it next to my body while floating in the bathroom, and then—a very important step—I turn on the air suction that flows through the flexible hose. The air suction replaces gravity, and it pulls the urine down the tube and into the waste tank hidden beneath the floor.

To use the toilet, I sit on the seat, adjust the leg restraints to keep myself from floating away, and then turn on the air suction and open the bowl. Again, air suction replaces gravity, and the waste is pulled into the bowl.

Astronauts working inside the shuttle dress much as they would on Earth. The temperature is controlled automatically, and there is plenty of air to breathe, so we do not need helmets or face masks. Our clothes are designed to be loose and comfortable and have plenty of big pockets. We put books, spoons, scissors, tape recorders, tools, and even bags of nuts in our pockets; if we simply laid them down, they would float away.

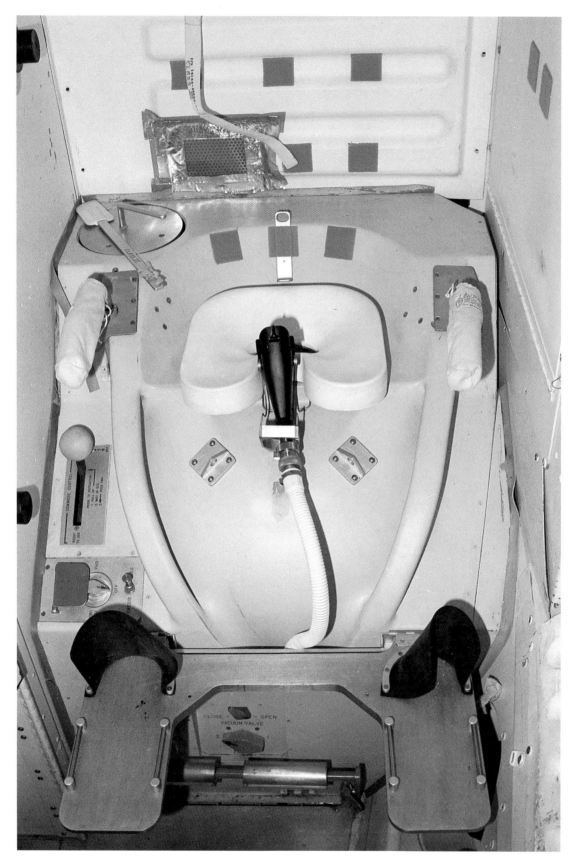

I keep my clothes in a locker, which is like a dresser drawer big enough to hold clean underwear, pants, shorts, and shirts. Getting dressed while weightless can be challenging. At first I found it difficult to pull on socks while tumbling in midair. Once I was used to it, though, I could put on my pants both legs at a time, which I can't do on Earth.

Astronauts do not wear boots or shoes while in orbit. When we are weightless, our feet are near the ceiling as often as they are near the floor, and it's easy to kick someone by accident. To avoid hurting each other, we either go barefoot or wear socks or slippers. We can't walk on the floor, so we don't need foot protection anyway. If we need to hold ourselves in place while we get clothes out of a locker or conduct an experiment, we just hook a toe into one of the foot loops attached to the shuttle's floor and walls. We don't need shoes with suction cups or magnets—in fact, we're glad not to have them, because it's much more fun to float.

Every day the crew polishes the computer terminals and vacuums the filters that keep our air clean. House-keeping in the space shuttle is a big job. Weightless dust, hair, and crumbs do not settle on the floor—they drift all over the cabin. Spilled coffee or juice floats around in globs until it collides with a wall or clogs one of the air filters. Making a mess is even easier in space than it is at home, and cleaning up is, unfortunately, much harder.

Kathy Sullivan having a problem with some film.

Astronauts are sent into space to launch new satellites into orbit, to return orbiting satellites to Earth, to fix broken satellites, and to perform many different types of scientific experiments.

The space shuttle carries satellites into orbit in its cargo bay. Satellites may be as small as a basketball or as large as a bus. Most are designed to be released from the spaceplane; a few are retrieved before the shuttle returns to Earth, but generally they are left in orbit to do their jobs. Some relay television signals across the country, some point telescopes at distant stars, and some aim weather cameras back at Earth.

It is not an easy job to launch a satellite. Before a flight, astronauts practice every step over and over so that they will be able to release the satellite at exactly the right time, at exactly the right spot over the Earth, and with the shuttle pointing in exactly the right direction. During the countdown to the satellite launch, the crew works as a team—a very well trained team working very closely together. Each astronaut "plays a position" on the flight deck: two are seated (wearing seatbelts to avoid floating away from the computers at a critical moment), one is near the windows, and one is floating behind the seats near the satellite switches.

A communications satellite just after launch from the shuttle. An astronaut inside the shuttle turned on the satellite to make sure it was still working after the shock of our launch from Earth and started it spinning on its table. Then the clamps that held the satellite were released, and the crew felt a dull thump as the spinning satellite popped up out of the shuttle. The satellite has rockets that will carry it into a much higher orbit after it is safely clear of the space shuttle. *Next page:* The space shuttle is photographed by a satellite that has just been released by the robot arm.

My calculator floats within easy reach on the flight deck.

What kind of scientific experiments do we conduct in space? We observe the stars and the Earth from our position two hundred miles up. On some flights we carry telescopes outside in the cargo bay. Because our orbit is above the atmosphere, these telescopes get a clearer view of the sun, stars, planets, and galaxies than any telescope on Earth. On some flights we carry sensitive cameras to take pictures of the land, sea, and weather back on Earth. Information gathered at shuttle height can help scientists study storms, air pollution, and volcanic eruptions and learn more about the planet we live on.

Inside the space shuttle, astronauts perform experiments exploring ways to make new substances—medicines, metals, or crystals—in weightlessness. We also record data about our own bodies to help scientists understand the effects of weightlessness. Before astronauts can set out on a two-year trip to Mars, scientists must be able to predict what will happen to people who stay in space that long.

Steve Hawley is recording experimental data for scientists back on Earth.

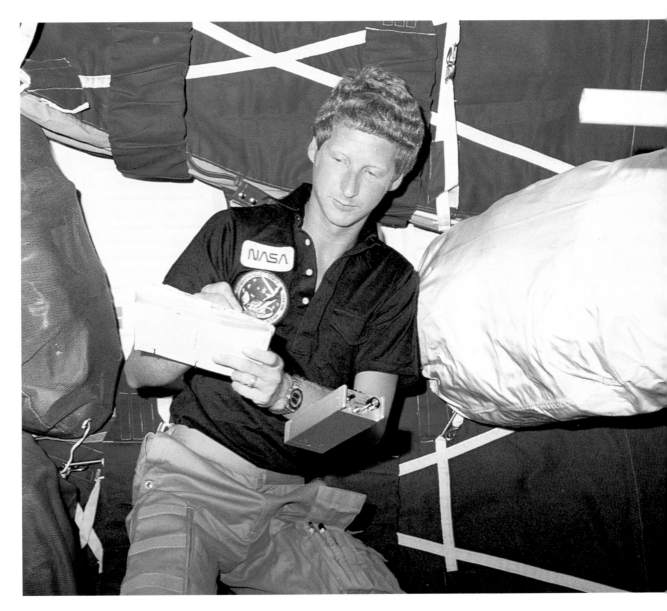

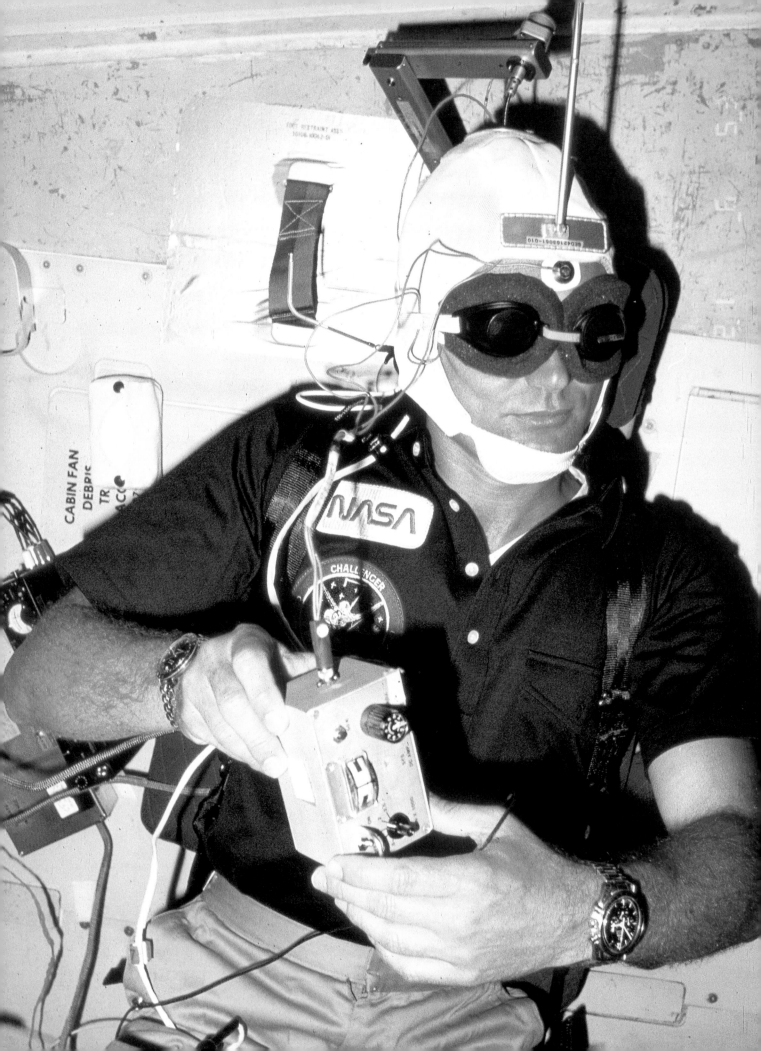

Left: Norm Thagard is wearing equipment that measures eye movements and reflexes in space. *Below:* Rhea Seddon is measuring Jake Garn's blood pressure to learn how the body changes in weightlessness.

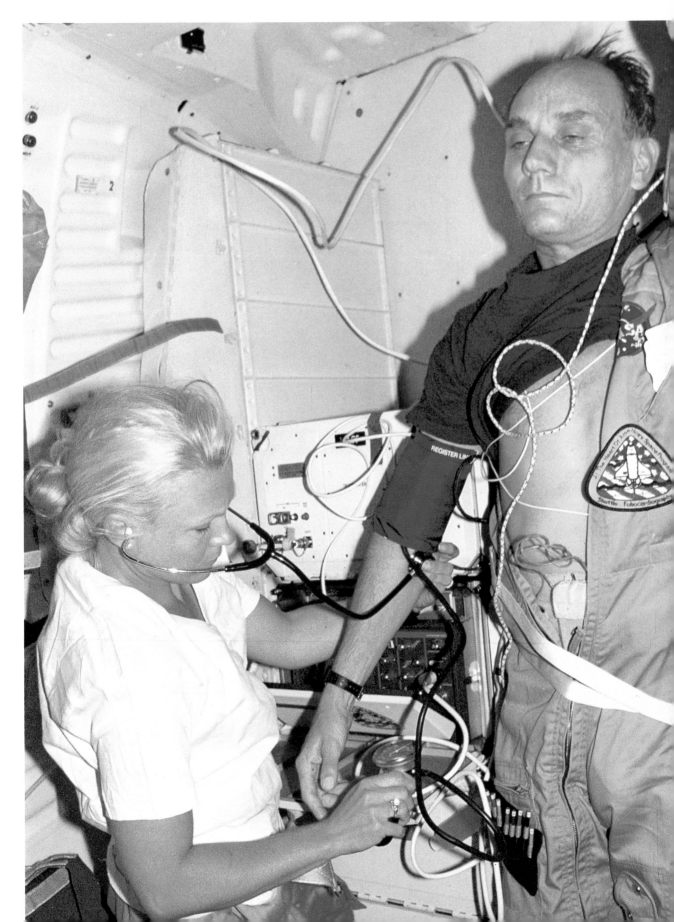

Astronauts are also sent into space to rendezvous with satellites already in orbit. We fly the space shuttle to within a few feet of a satellite, capture it with the robot arm, put it into the cargo bay, and bring it and its data back down to Earth with us. A broken satellite may be repaired on the shuttle and returned to orbit.

Rendezvous with a satellite also requires hours upon hours of practice—plus very close cooperation and teamwork. One astronaut has to fly the spaceplane to the satellite, another keeps track of the location of both, and a third controls the robot arm. This takes several hours of hard work, but it's the only way to bring a valuable satellite back to Earth.

Most of our work can be done inside the space shuttle, but sometimes we have to go outside, either to make repairs or to perform an experiment. While we are inside, we are protected from the emptiness of outer space, but outside there is no air to breathe, and the temperature can be very hot or very cold. To leave the protection of the space shuttle, we have to put on spacesuits.

We use cameras constantly—to take pictures of the Earth, of experiments, of satellites, and of each other.

We carry two spacesuits in the shuttle's airlock, a small room between the mid-deck and the cargo bay that can be sealed off from the main cabin and opened into space. On every spacewalk, two astronauts go outside together because it is easier and safer to work along with someone else in that strange environment. While two astronauts go spacewalking, the other three stay inside to watch over the space shuttle.

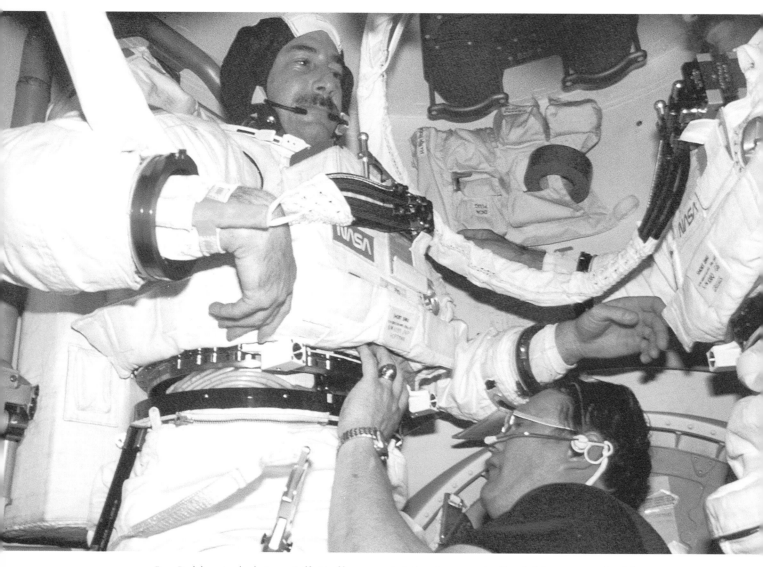

Bo Bobko is helping Jeff Hoffman get into the top half of his spacesuit. The switches and dials on the front of the spacesuit help them make sure that the suit is working right.

Astronauts who will go outside begin getting dressed several hours ahead of time. First they put on something that looks like long underwear but is made of elastic with rubber tubes sewn into it. Water will flow through these tubes to keep the astronauts cool since their body heat has no way to dissipate once they are sealed into their spacesuits.

Next the spacewalkers pull on the lower halves of their spacesuits. The bottom is all in one piece: big, rigid boots attached to bulky, flexible insulated pants. On Earth the astronauts would have to lie on the floor to wriggle into the pants. In space they can slip into them while floating in the mid-deck.

The spacewalkers float into the airlock and slide into the upper halves of their suits. The upper half, which is mounted on the airlock wall, is a hard shell with flexible arms. The astronaut's head sticks out through a metal ring at the neck, where the helmet will be connected, and the hands stick out through two metal rings where gloves will attach. This part of the spacesuit is very heavy on Earth. It holds the oxygen supply, the water, the fans, and the batteries that run the fans and pumps that keep the astronaut alive during a spacewalk.

When the spacewalking partners are inside their suits on the airlock wall, another astronaut (one of those who will stay inside) helps lock the pieces of each suit together. Before putting on helmets, the astronauts put on "Snoopy caps" that have radio speakers inside the earflaps and microphones that stick out in front of their mouths so that they can talk with each other and with the rest of the crew.

At last they are ready to put on helmets and big, awkward gloves. First they brush their hair back, adjust their caps, and scratch their noses one last time. They won't be able to do these things again until the spacewalk is over.

The astronaut who has been helping leaves the airlock and closes the hatch. In their bulky suits the two spacewalkers almost fill the small space. They wait alone in the airlock for several minutes while the air is gradually pumped out. They can feel their ears popping as they wait for the pressure gauge to show that the air is gone.

Finally they can open the hatch and reach out into space. Before they float out of the airlock, they have to hook their tethers—thin wires attached to their suits—to the space shuttle. The tethers keep the astronauts from drifting away from the spaceplane. Although the astronauts stay hooked to the shuttle, they can move freely at the end of the lines.

Floating out into space, the spacewalking astronauts become human satellites. *They* are orbiting Earth! Their view stretches from horizon to horizon and across the whole sky. They don't need the space shuttle, at least for a while, because their spacesuits have enough air and battery power to keep them alive for about seven hours. There is even a food stick and a drink bag of water inside each helmet.

Wearing the jetpack, which is like a chair that attaches to the spacesuit, an astronaut can fly hundreds of feet away from the shuttle. Bruce McCandless uses hand controls in the armrests to maneuver in space.

They move into the shuttle's cargo bay, their tethers reeling out behind them like fishing lines. All the tools they need during a spacewalk are kept in a big tool chest in the cargo bay. They remove the ones they want and hook them to their wrists or waists. As the spacewalkers float slowly around the bay, they look like octopuses, with wrenches and screwdrivers floating like tentacles from their spacesuits.

To stand still in one spot, they lock their boots into special foot holders like ski bindings that are attached to the shuttle.

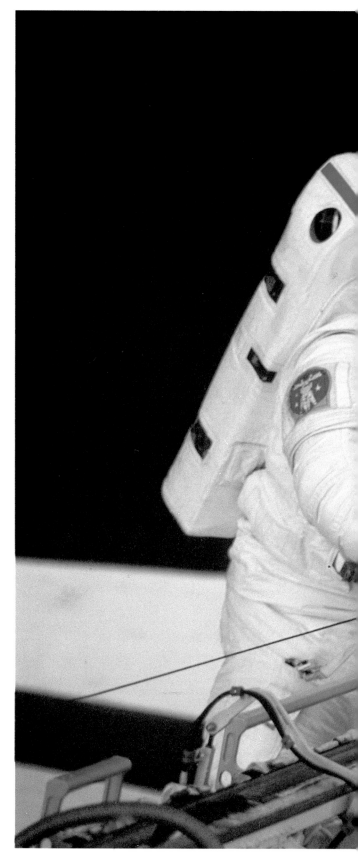

Dave Griggs working outside.

An astronaut can even stand at the end of the robot arm while a crewmember inside the shuttle moves the arm around.

When the sun shines on them, spacewalkers can feel its warmth through their gloves. But when their hands are in the shade, or when the shuttle reaches the dark side of Earth, they cool off quickly.

Working in a spacesuit is not easy. An astronaut's fingers, hands, and arms get tired because every move that is made—even opening and closing a gloved hand—requires pushing against part of the spacesuit from inside.

When an astronaut rides on the robot arm, feet are locked into a foot holder, tools and bags are out in front, and the arm is moved about from place to place by another astronaut inside the shuttle. *Next page:* Repairing a satellite from the robot arm.

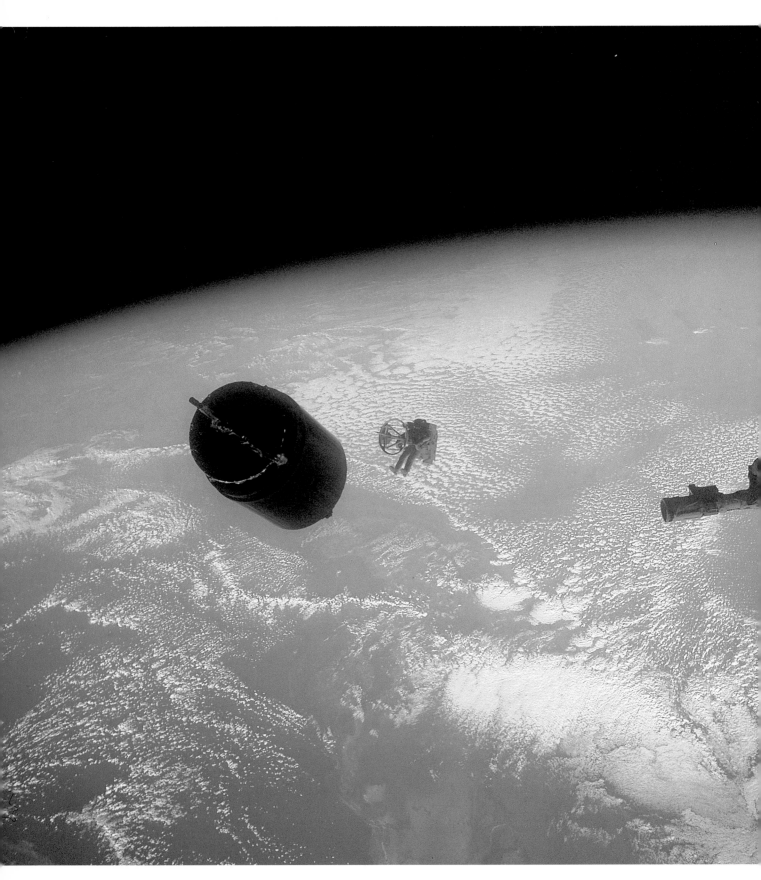

Dale Gardner, wearing a jetpack, has just gone to capture a broken satellite and bring it back to the shuttle. The satellite was launched to relay TV and telephone signals, but its rockets failed to put it into high orbit.

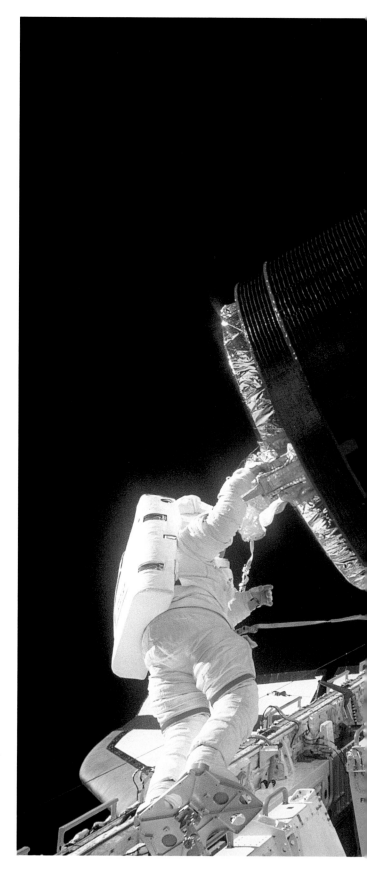

Once the satellite is near the shuttle, the astronauts wrestle it into the cargo bay. Even though it would weigh 2,000 pounds on Earth, it is weightless in space. Joe Allen easily holds it above his head, but it's big and awkward to control, like a huge balloon.

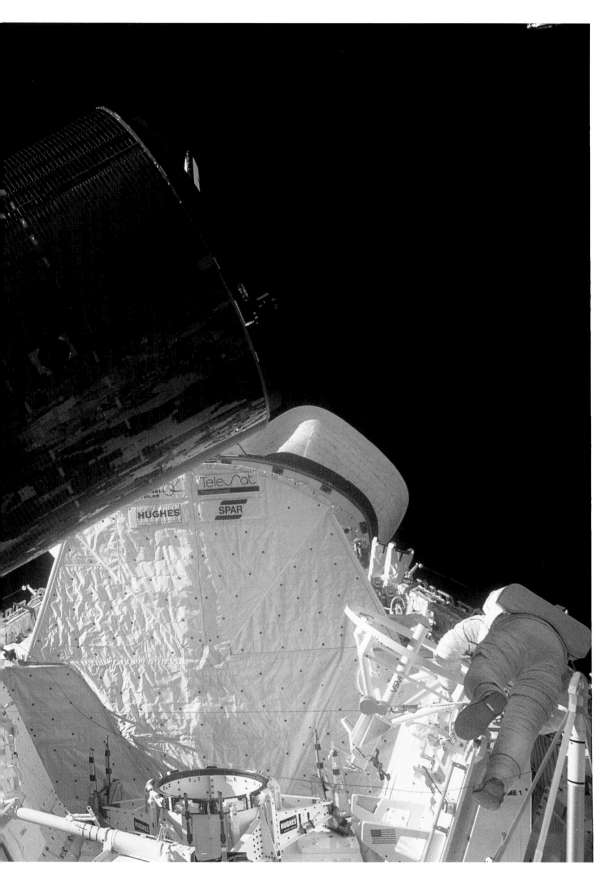

When it's time to rejoin the rest of the crew inside the spaceplane, after several hours outside, the spacewalkers float back into the airlock. But even though they may be tired, they pause to take one last look at the view of Earth and sky before they close the door on outer space.

Jim van Hoften and Pinky Nelson are working to repair a broken satellite. After it is repaired it will be released from the space shuttle.

THE DAY BEFORE THE SHUTTLE RETURNS TO EARTH, astronauts have to put away all loose equipment. Cameras, food trays, and books will stay attached to the ceiling or walls with Velcro as long as they are weightless, but they would come crashing to the floor if we left them out during re-entry. We drift around collecting things and stowing them in drawers. An amazing number of lost pencils and books turn up floating behind wall and ceiling panels.

Immediately after launch we folded and put away all but two of our seats to give us more room inside. Now we have to reattach them to the floor so we can sit in them during re-entry. We must also find the suits, boots, helmets, and life vests that we haven't worn since launch and put them on again for landing. It is often hard to remember where we stored everything. Once I almost had to come back to Earth barefoot because I had forgotten where I had put my boots!

Four or five hours before landing, we begin to drink liquid—four or more big glasses each—and take salt pills to keep the liquid in our bodies. We have to do this because our bodies have gotten rid of some water during the flight to adjust to weightlessness. Now we are about to feel Earth's gravity again, and if we do not replace the lost fluid ahead of time, we will feel very thirsty and lightheaded—and maybe even pass out—as gravity pulls the fluid in our bodies toward our legs.

We also put on "g-suits," pants that can be inflated to

keep the blood from pooling in our legs. If we begin to feel lightheaded as we re-enter the atmosphere, a sign that not enough blood is reaching the brain, we can in-flate our g-suits.

Finally we strap ourselves into our seats, connect our helmets to the oxygen supply, and fire the shuttle's small space engines. This "de-orbit burn" slows the shuttle down and brings us back into Earth's atmosphere. Once the engines are fired to start re-entry, there is no turning back.

The space shuttle re-enters the atmosphere about thirty minutes later. It is moving very fast, and as it col-lides with molecules of gas in the air it becomes very hot—in places, over twenty-five hundred degrees Fahr-enheit. Only the special heat tiles glued on the outside of the spaceplane keep it from melting. The tiles protect the shuttle so well that inside we do not even feel the heat. But we can tell that it is very hot outside, because all we can see through the windows is a bright, flickering orange glow from the hot air around us.

After we have traveled a short distance down into the atmosphere, we begin to hear the rushing of wind as we shoot through the thin air. We feel a little vibration, like what passengers might feel on a slightly bumpy airplane ride. Gravity slowly begins pulling us into our seats, and we start to feel heavier and heavier. Since we are used to weightless books, pencils, arms, and heads, all these things now seem very heavy to us. It's an effort even to lift a hand.

This is what the pilot sees out the window just moments before landing: the space shuttle runway. The four lights in a row in the water, at the bottom of the picture, help guide the pilot down to a safe landing.

As the shuttle falls farther down into the atmosphere, it flies less and less like a spacecraft and more and more like an airplane. It gradually stops using its small space jets to maneuver and starts using the control surfaces on its tail and wings instead. These surfaces were useless in

84

the vacuum of space, but they become more effective as the air thickens. When the shuttle is about as low as most airplanes fly, it is only a few miles from the runway and is traveling below the speed of sound. At this point it is flying like a glider—an airplane with no engines.

Until this stage of re-entry the computers have been flying the spaceplane, but now the commander takes control. We approach the runway much more steeply than we would in an ordinary airplane, and we feel almost as if we're flying straight down. We slide forward in our seats, held back only by our shoulder harnesses, as the shuttle dives toward the ground. The pilot lowers the landing gear when the spaceplane is only a few hundred feet above the ground. The landing gear slows us down, but we still land at about two hundred miles per hour—quite a bit faster than most airplanes. The rear wheels touch the runway first, so gently that inside we can't even be sure we've landed. Then the nose wheel comes down with a hard thump, and we know we're back on Earth.

A few hundred feet above the runway, the pilot lowers the spaceplane's landing gear. These wheels have been tucked up into the belly of the shuttle since before it went out to the launch pad.

The space shuttle rolls to a stop. As I unstrap myself from my seat and try to stand up, I am amazed at how heavy my whole body feels. My arms, my head, my neck—each part of me seems to be made of lead. It is hard to stand straight, it is hard to lift my legs to walk, and it is hard to carry my helmet and books. I start down the ladder from the flight deck to the mid-deck— the same ladder that was unnecessary just an hour ago—and I have to concentrate just to place my feet on the rungs. My muscles are nearly as strong as they were before the one-week space flight, but my brain expects everything to be light and easy to lift.

My heart, too, has gotten used to weightlessness. For several days, it has not had to pump blood up from my legs against gravity. Now it is working harder again, and for several minutes after we land it beats much faster than normal.

My sense of balance also needs to adjust to gravity. For a few minutes I feel dizzy every time I move my head. I have trouble keeping my balance or walking in a straight line for about fifteen minutes after landing.

We stay inside the spaceplane for a little while to give ourselves a chance to get over these strange sensations. We do knee bends and practice walking while the ground crew moves a boarding platform over to the shuttle and opens the hatch. Then a doctor comes on board to make sure everyone is in shape to get off. We are all still a little wobbly, but about thirty minutes after landing we are ready to climb out of the space shuttle and walk down the stairs to the runway.

Once my feet are on the ground, I look back and admire the space shuttle. I take a few moments to get used to being back on Earth and to say goodbye to the plane that took us to space and back.

I WANT TO THANK THE MANY PEOPLE AT NASA WHO GAVE me their cooperation and assistance. Special thanks go to NASA space shuttle astronauts: Joseph P. Allen, James P. Bagian, John E. Blaha, Guion S. Bluford, Karol J. Bobko, Charles F. Bolden, Vance D. Brand, Daniel C. Brandenstein, Roy D. Bridges, Jr., James F. Buchli, Franklin Chang-Diaz, Mary L. Cleave, Michael L. Coats, Richard O. Covey, John O. Creighton, Robert L. Crippen, Bonnie J. Dunbar, Anthony W. England, Joe H. Engle, John M. Fabian, Anna L. Fisher, William F. Fisher, C. Gordon Fullerton, Dale A. Gardner, Guy S. Gardner, Owen K. Garriott, Robert L. Gibson, Ronald J. Grabe, Frederick D. Gregory, S. David Griggs, Terry J. Hart, Henry W. Hartsfield, Frederick H. Hauck, Steven A. Hawley, Karl G. Henize, David C. Hilmers, Jeffrey A. Hoffman, David D. Leestma, Bill Lenoir, Don L. Lind, John M. Lounge, Jack Lousma, Shannon W. Lucid, Thomas K. Mattingly, Jon A. McBride, Bruce McCandless II, Ronald E. McNair, Richard M. Mullane, Story F. Musgrave, Steven Nagel, George D. Nelson, Claude Nicollier, Bryan D. O'Connor, Ellison S. Onizuka, Robert F. Overmyer, Robert A. Parker, Donald H. Peterson, Judith A. Resnik, Richard N. Richards, Jerry L. Ross, Francis R. Scobee, M. Rhea Seddon, Brewster H. Shaw, Jr., Loren J. Shriver, Michael J. Smith, Sherwood C. Spring, Robert C. Springer, Robert Stewart, Kathryn D. Sullivan, Norman E. Thagard, William E. Thornton, Richard H. Truly, James D. van Hoften, David M. Walker, Paul J. Weitz, Donald E. Williams, John W. Young.

GLOSSARY

ACCESS ARM: The part of the launch tower surrounding the space shuttle that allows astronauts to walk from an elevator on the launch pad to the shuttle's entrance hatch.

AIRLOCK: A small chamber located between the shuttle's mid-deck and cargo bay, which can be sealed off and slowly emptied of air until the pressure in the chamber is as low as that outside in space.

ATMOSPHERE: The gases surrounding a planet. Earth's atmosphere is made up mostly of nitrogen (79%) and oxygen (20%).

CARGO BAY: A large, open area of the space shuttle, which is used to hold satellites and scientific equipment. It is covered by two large doors during takeoff and re-entry. The doors are open while the shuttle is in orbit.

COMPUTER TERMINALS: Screens that display information for the crew. With the terminals are keyboards that the astronauts use to talk to the shuttle's computers.

DE-ORBIT BURN: The firing of space engines to slow the shuttle and bring it out of its orbit and back into the Earth's atmosphere.

ESCAPE HARNESSES: Vests that astronauts wear over their flight suits during launch and landing. Each vest has a ring that can be hooked to a rope so the astronaut can slide from the space shuttle to the ground in case of an emergency after landing.

FILTERS: Mesh screens that trap dust and dirt, which would otherwise circulate in the air inside the space shuttle.

FLIGHT DECK: One of the two rooms inside the space shuttle. It is located above the mid-deck and contains the controls for the space shuttle, for the robot arm, and for most experiments.

FLIGHT SUITS: One-piece suits worn by astronauts on the shuttle during launch and landing. Unlike spacesuits, flight suits are not pressurized and would not allow an astronaut to survive outside the shuttle.

G'S: A term used for measuring gravitational force, as in "3 g's" or "0 g." "1 g" means a gravitational force equal to that felt on Earth.

G-SUIT: Inflatable pants worn by an astronaut during the shuttle's re-entry into Earth's atmosphere. When inflated, the g-suit presses on leg veins to help push blood up into the body, enabling the heart to pump enough blood to the brain.

HATCH: An airtight doorway in the space shuttle.

HEAT TILES: Special tiles on the outside of the shuttle that absorb heat during re-entry and prevent the heat from reaching the metal skin of the spaceplane.

HORIZON: Where Earth and sky appear to meet.

LAUNCH ENGINES (also called **MAIN ENGINES**): Three powerful engines that burn liquid hydrogen and liquid oxygen to help lift the shuttle into space.

MID-DECK: The larger of the two rooms inside the space shuttle where astronauts live during a flight. It contains the lockers that hold food and clothes, the kitchen area, and the space toilet.

MISSION CONTROL: The room at Houston's Lyndon B. Johnson Space Center where NASA engineers monitor each space flight and issue instructions to its crew.

NASA: Abbreviation for the National Aeronautics and Space Administration, the United States government agency that plans and operates space flights.

ORBIT: A path that an object follows around a planet or star, without having to use engines, because the force of gravity is pulling the object toward the planet's or star's surface. For example, the Earth orbits the sun; the space shuttle orbits the Earth.

RE-ENTRY: The last part of a space flight, when the space shuttle leaves its orbit in space and returns to Earth's atmosphere.

RENDEZVOUS: The French word for "meeting," which is used to refer to a meeting in space between the shuttle and a satellite.

ROBOT ARM: A huge electrical crane shaped much like a human arm. It is operated by an astronaut inside the shuttle and used to place satellites into orbit or to pull satellites out of orbit.

SATELLITE: An object that orbits another object in space. The word is often used to refer to something built to orbit the Earth (for example, "communications satellites" which transmit television signals, "weather satellites" which take photographs, etc.).

SOLID ROCKETS: Rockets that burn solid fuel. Two powerful solid rocket boosters are used to help get the shuttle into space.

SPACE ENGINES: Small engines that are used by the shuttle after it is outside Earth's atmosphere. These engines are also called the Orbital Maneuvering System, and are the engines used for the "de-orbit burn."

SPACE SICKNESS: Uncomfortable sensations experienced by some astronauts during their first two days in space, caused by the body's adjustment to weightlessness.

SPACESUITS: Pressurized suits that astronauts put on to walk in space. The suits control temperature and supply oxygen to astronauts, allowing them to survive in space outside the shuttle for several hours.

TETHERS: Lines that connect spacewalking astronauts to the shuttle.

TREADMILL: An exercise machine that allows an astronaut to run in place and get some exercise while in orbit.

WEIGHTLESSNESS: The word used to describe the condition in which all objects float in space. When weightless it may seem as though we are not subject to the earth's gravitational pull, but in fact it is gravity constantly pulling toward the center of the earth that keeps us in orbit.

INDEX